Rottweiler Training Guide

How to Train a Rottweiler, Including Rottweiler Breed-Specific Training Tips and Techniques

by Leanna Holst

Table of Contents

Introduction

Are you the proud owner of a Rottweiler? Or perhaps you and your family are planning on getting a Rottweiler puppy? Also called Rotties or Rotts, Rottweilers are among the most favored breeds of dogs that people choose to have as pets and companions. This is likely because they are often good-natured, obedient, and gentle dogs. They are said to be descendants of the Roman drover dog and relatives of the Italian Mastiff, making them good working dogs who are great helpers for their owners. In olden times, Rotts were used for herding cattle, but in the present day, they are more often utilized as guard dogs, police dogs, guide dogs, and rescue dogs.

If you are thinking of raising a dog from this magnificent breed, you should be prepared to train it. Rotties make amazing pets and companion dogs. However, they can become a handful and can even cause problems in your home if not properly trained. A number of Rottweiler owners hire professional dog trainers to train their dogs, however, with sufficient knowledge, anybody can train their Rottweilers without spending a lot of money for such dog training services.

It's unfortunate that not all Rott owners have the necessary know-how required to train their dogs, as Rottweilers learn quite fast and, with proper training, can become very useful to their owners. This book will give Rottweiler owners useful tips on how to train their Rottweiler puppies and correct bad behavior in adult Rottweiler dogs. Is your Rottweiler disobeying your commands, ignoring you, or showing aggressive behavior towards people? Here, you can read all that you need to know about training your dog: from teaching it to follow simple commands to ensuring that you have a happy and well-behaved dog.

Inside you'll find issues Rottweiler owners usually encounter plus the common mistakes that owners make while training their dog. But most importantly, you'll find information on how to properly train your dog. Training your Rottweiler is vital, but it does not have to be a daunting task for you or an unpleasant experience for your pet. When done properly, Rottweiler training can be fun and rewarding for both the owner and the dog. This is crucial, since training your dog is an ongoing commitment that you should be willing to do daily for as long as you plan to own a Rottweiler. It takes a lot of effort and patience to train a Rottweiler but with this book, you have all that you need to know in order to teach your dog not only new tricks, but so much more!

5

Chapter 1: Starting the Training Early

Although there are some folks that prefer to buy adult Rotties that have already been trained by previous owners, most people who want to own a Rottweiler get them as puppies. Professional dog trainers as well as Rottweiler owners can tell you that the best time to train your dog is when they are still young, preferably between the ages of six weeks to six months. This is the period when puppies are the most receptive and malleable, and thus it's the best time for them to learn about obedience. Although it is still possible to start training a Rott that is older than six months, you will have the most success if training starts at a young age. You'll need more time, effort, and patience in training older dogs than younger ones, but the things we are about to discuss in this guide are all important when training a Rottweiler of any age.

Rottweilers are known for being intelligent, so you don't really need to worry about there being any difficulty teaching yours how to follow commands. Keep in mind that these big dogs were specifically bred to be working dogs, so they are naturally obedient and loyal to their masters. At the end of the day, Rotties want to please you and make you happy, so never lose your temper when your dog becomes unruly. When training a young puppy or even an older Rottweiler, it is important to use only positive reinforcement. This is really the best way to teach not only Rottweilers, but dogs of any age or breed.

If you want a cute, small, and cuddly lapdog for a pet, then a Rottweiler is probably not the dog for you. Rottweilers are a large breed of dog and can weigh as much as a hundred and fifty pounds. They also have a tendency to become overweight, especially when you're using food as a reward to train them. This is actually one of the reasons why you need to train your Rott early in their life. You don't want a big, heavy, rowdy, and disobedient dog reigning in your home. Train your Rott as early as possible so that they will be easier to manage when they inevitably become large and strong. Most importantly, this will help them grow into a useful and helpful dog.

Socialization is also very important for Rottweilers, so the younger they get used to people and other dogs, the better. Rotties can become very territorial and protective of their master and their home, so if they are not trained to socialize with other people and other dogs, they can become a problem. Rotts who are not socialized at an early age may attack those visiting your home, including young children and other dogs that they meet. But when a Rott is exposed to other people and other dogs very early in their life, they are more apt to be playful and friendly. If their territorial nature can be curbed, then they will learn how to distinguish normal behavior from suspicious and possibly threatening behavior.

Chapter 2: Understanding Dominance

A Rottweiler owner must understand the concept of dominance when it comes to training dogs. In dominance-based training, the trainer or the dog owner continually creates rules that the dog must obey. This kind of training helps to establish that the dog owner is the leader and that their dog is the follower and never the other way around.

In dominance-based dog training, it should be emphasized that physical force should never be used. A lot of dog owners think that hitting or shouting at their dog will result in obedience, but this simply isn't true. Hitting your dog when they do not obey your command can be detrimental to your training because they might develop fear towards you. It is important to remember that fear is not the same as submission; a fearful dog is likely to reject learning commands. Shouting is also not very helpful because it will only confuse your dog, as they may not even understand the reason why you are shouting. With this kind of training, it is very important to remain kind and patient with your dog. You can establish leadership without hurting your dog and making them fear you.

Some Rottweilers can develop dominant behavior and may try to assert themselves over their owners, but you don't need to worry because that is natural in dogs and it can be fixed with some tried and tested methods. The first thing you should do is try to better understand your dog's behavior by being more observant. Find out why your dog is behaving the way they do. Are they challenging you or being aggressive? Perhaps, he is feeling threatened by something in your home? Is it a guest, perhaps, or something new in your house that he is unfamiliar with? Figure out the stimulus to each of your dog's behavioral responses, so you can remove things in his environment that trigger bad behavior. Look out for signs of stress or anxiety in your dog, and find out what's behind his dominant or aggressive conduct. Once the cause of his aggression is removed, your dog will be grateful and will be happy to follow your commands. Understanding your dog's behavior will undoubtedly help a great deal in your training.

Many Rottweilers develop dominant behavior partly because their owners fail to train them properly. For instance, some dog owners are not consistent when it comes to implementing their training rules, and at times, they let their dogs break the rules. Never allow your dog to lead and you to follow them. Be consistent and show your dog that rules are rules and you don't back down when challenged.

Don't slack off when it comes to training your Rottie. Always remember that dog training is a continuous process, and dog owners must always stand by the rules they have set for their dog.

Chapter 3: Socializing Your Rottweiler

Do you keep your Rottweiler locked inside the house all day as you work from home? Do you take your dog for regular walks and allow her to meet other dogs at the park? Socialization is crucial to a Rottweiler's training because, just like other breeds of canines, Rotts need to become familiar and comfortable around other people and other animals.

There are a myriad of ways to socialize your Rottie: Take your dog with you when you go for a run. Bring her to the park so she can meet other dogs. Let your friends come over to visit you and allow your dog to play around with them. If it's okay with your friends, you can also bring your dog with you when you drop by their homes. It's important to expose your dog to people and other animals so that she can get used to them, be familiar with them, and feel comfortable around them.

Just like humans, dogs need to socialize for fun as well. This means that your dog needs socialization for more than just training; she needs it for her wellbeing as well. You will find yourself with a much happier pet if you let them run around the park and play with other dogs. Additionally, your Rottweiler can learn a lot from being in the company of other animals and other people. Rottweilers are intelligent dogs and are often used as guard dogs or police dogs. They are also trained as service dogs for those with certain handicaps, like the blind and epileptics. Therefore, when a Rottweiler is exposed to various situations and placed in the company of different people and animals, he will learn to distinguish normal behavior from abnormal or threatening behavior. He will be able to tell which situations are safe and which are dangerous. Socialization plays a vital role in the development of all breeds of dogs, but this is especially true when it comes to Rottweilers since many of them play such a vital social role. Proper socialization will help mold them into well-adjusted and well-behaved dogs.

When it comes to socializing Rotts, the main role of the owner is to make sure that their dogs' social experiences are pleasant and comfortable. Good socialization experiences will build the dog's confidence, but unpleasant outings and meetings will only make your dog fearful and he may not want to repeat the activity again. So be sure to make the walks in the park pleasant for your dog and always be mindful when you let your dog meet other people. Recall when we briefly mentioned the importance of socializing your Rott early in the first chapter. Young Rottweilers need to be socially trained so that they can become good pets and home companions. Some Rotties that are not socialized properly have a tendency to become anxious when visitors come over, and they may become aggressive towards children and other people they aren't familiar with.

One of the joys of owning a pet is having a companion with you all the time, so be sure to take your Rottweiler with you everywhere you go if you can. Take her to the park, the beach, and take her whenever you go for a walk. Let people meet her and pet her. Allow her to play with other dogs and even meet cats. Rottweilers are gentle dogs, and they can become quite friendly with new faces and other pets if they are socialized at a young age. You can also make use of the time spent socializing your dog to meet other dog owners and talk about your Rottweilers.

Chapter 4: Training with Positive Reinforcement

The best way to train any kind of pet, whether they are a dog, cat, or even a bird, is to use positive reinforcement. Rottweilers are no exception. They learn commands better when positive reinforcement is used. Positive reinforcement means rewarding good behavior to reinforce it. Compare this to negative reinforcement, which is punishing bad behavior to discourage it. This is a much more unreliable technique as it has a good chance of making your dog fearful and untrusting.

How is positive reinforcement used to train a Rott? All you need to do is to reward your dog whenever he displays good behavior. When your dog does something that you like such as following a command, you give him a treat or praise. By doing so, your dog will understand that that specific behavior will result in a reward. The next time, he will remember the command, his action, and the treat or reward that comes after it. This is how your dog will learn. As a dog owner, you should know that dogs cannot understand any human language and he will probably not understand you when you talk to him. However, he will understand that certain behavior results in rewards. Your Rottie may not pick up on your commands right away, so remember to be patient with your dog. Repeat your commands gently, and again, be patient. Don't shout at your dog or feel frustrated when he doesn't obey commands or repeat a certain behavior that he successfully displayed just a few minutes ago. Training a Rottweiler, or any dog for that matter, requires a lot of time, effort, and again, a load of patience. You should also always remember to train your dog in a loving yet firm manner.

Communicating with your pet Rottweiler cannot be done with words because, as mentioned before, dogs cannot understand human language. However, by using positive reinforcement, you are communicating with your Rottie in a language that he can actually understand. Your dog repeats a behavior and you reward him. He understands this and learns to associate certain types of behavior with positive occurrences and emotions. Take note, though, that rewards don't always have to be food or treats. It is possible that your Rottweiler will gain too much weight if you only reward them with dog treats. Instead of food, you can also give toys as rewards, or simply praise your dog when they get something right. Rottweilers are intelligent dogs so if they see that their behavior has resulted in their master smiling, laughing, or acting happy, that alone can be reward for these loving animals.

In order dog-training using positive reinforcement more effective, you need to give the reward right after your dog performs the act you were asking them to do. It should be immediate so that he can associate the reward with the behavior he showed. Remember to create a relaxed and pleasant training atmosphere for you and your dog. If he doesn't get it right today, try again tomorrow. There is no sense becoming stressed over training your Rottweiler. Take your time, and allow your dog to take his time, too. Before long, you'll have a well-behaved, fully-trained dog in your home.

Chapter 5: Common Training Mistakes to Avoid

Unlike professional dog trainers who most likely know everything when it comes to training Rotts, regular dog owners tend to make a lot of mistakes when training their dogs. Nevertheless, don't feel discouraged if you are a new Rottweiler owner, because there are proven ways to ensure you don't make these mistakes. Here are some of the most common mistakes that dog owners make when training their dogs and their respective solutions.

Not Rewarding or Disciplining Immediately

As explained in Chapter 4, in order to make your Rottweiler training effective, the reward must be given immediately after your dog displays the desired good behavior. If you delay the reward or fail to give it, your dog will not associate it with the behavior you wished him to display. As a result, he will not learn the command. It is the same with disciplining your Rottie or discouraging him from doing something unpleasant. You must always say a firm "No" right after he does the behavior you don't want him to do. Always be prompt with your reactions; reward good behavior immediately, and discourage bad behavior right away so your dog will associate the reward or the discouragement with the last behavior that he displayed. This means that if he committed a mistake or displayed bad behavior hours ago, you should not discipline him for it because he has likely forgotten about it. For instance, if you come home after being gone for hours and find that your puppy has gone to the bathroom in the house when he wasn't supposed to, there is no point in disciplining him as they won't associate the discipline with that action. On the opposite end of the training spectrum, do not reward your Rottie for something good that he did thirty minutes ago as he won't understand what you're rewarding him for. Only reward and discourage seconds after the behavior was displayed.

Punishment and Yelling

During the course of your dog's training, it is important that you avoid yelling and hitting your dog. These two actions will not help you train your Rottweiler. When trainers resort to physical discipline, dogs can reject the training altogether. They will become scared and discouraged, and they won't understand what you're yelling the same way they don't understand what you're saying when you're praising them, so try not to lose your patience when your Rottie fails to obey a command. If at any point during the training you feel frustrated or even downright angry, just stop and let your dog be for a while. Later, when you are ready again, try the same command and resume the training. Keep in mind that punishment is counterproductive to a Rottweiler's training and showing aggression towards your dog is never a good idea.

It's understandable that dog owners become exasperated when training their dogs; however, it is never acceptable to hit your dog. The only thing you can do when you get upset is to calm down and continue the training when you're more relaxed. When you show aggressive behavior towards your dog, they will just become afraid of you and they will stop attempting to follow any of your commands at all for fear of being punished.

Babying Your Rottweiler

Although many dog owners spoil and pamper their pets, it really isn't recommended if you wish to train your dog properly. Your dog may look irresistibly cute and at times you just want to horse around with her or coddle him, but keep in mind that you should never do that during training time. Don't allow your dog to jump on you or lie on top of you. It may seem like playing but it disrupts your dominance-based training. If you allow your dog to sit on top of you while you lie down on the floor, there's a chance that he will take this as a sign that he is the dominant one in your relationship. There is also the possibility that your dog will be frightened in certain situations, such as during thunderstorms or fireworks displays, but you still shouldn't baby him under those circumstances. Just show him that everything is normal and he will naturally adjust to the situation.

Pulling and Jerking the Leash

Training your Rottweiler to walk with a leash is one of the most necessary aspects of their training. However, there are many mistakes people make when it comes to leash training. For instance, many dog owners play a kind of tug-of-war game with their dogs. This is a mistake because in dominance-based training, you always have to lead and the dog always has to follow. When you let your Rottie pull you in another direction, you become the follower and your dog becomes the leader. So what you need to do is to stand firm when your dog starts pulling on the leash. Don't pull back, just stand where you are for a while until your Rottweiler realizes that she cannot pull you in the direction she wants and that you will not budge when pulled.

Talking to Your Dog

It has become a habit of pet owners to talk to their pets like they would with a neighbor, a roommate, or a friend. However, you shouldn't do this during training as Rottweilers cannot understand the human language and they will only become confused about what you want from them. The more words you use to address him during training, the more perplexed your dog will become. For example if you are trying to train your puppy to sit by saying: "Come on boy. Sit for Mommy. Come on, come on. You can sit can, can't you? Sit, boy, sit," then that will just be counterproductive to what you're actually trying to accomplish. Your dog most likely didn't understand anything in that long string of words. Just say "Sit" when you want your Rottie to sit. Don't add other words as that will only confuse your dog.

Training your Rottweiler can be very challenging and time-consuming. However, when your Rottie is already trained and well-behaved, you will finally reap the benefits of your efforts, and just the experience of successfully training and working with your dog will be very satisfying and rewarding in and of itself.

Chapter 6: Teaching Simple Commands

While many will think that dog training is only comprised of teaching your dogs a few tricks, that is really not the case. Training your Rottweiler starts from a very young age and the process continues even when your dog is already ten or twelve years old. Training is composed of so much more than just teaching your dog how to sit, stay, and roll over. Nevertheless, these simple commands are the very first things that a dog will need to learn. When your Rottweiler is able to learn simple commands, he will be more obedient and easier to manage overall.

Teach Your Dog to "Sit"

Your Rottweiler will grow up to be a very large dog. Teaching her to sit can make your life so much easier. To teach your dog to sit, first grab her attention. Calling her name is one way, while others may choose to clap their hands loudly instead. Choose whatever works for you and your Rott. When your dog's attention is on you, clearly and distinctly say the word "sit." Give her time to follow your command. Repeat the command until she responds. Try not to push your dog down to teach her how to sit. One method of teaching her how to respond to the word "sit" is by holding a treat in front of her and slowly raising it above her head. Her head will follow the treat up until she is forced to sit to keep track of it. Once she is in the desired sitting position, reward her with a treat, a toy, or some other form of praise when she accomplishes it. To ensure that she associates the word "sit" with that position, see if she responds to the word without the treat. If after many tries your dog does not respond to the training, stop, and try again later.

Hand Me Your "Paw"

Others say, "Shake hands" or "Give me your paw". However, remember that the more words you use, the more confused your dog will be, so it's really better to just say one-word commands. Say, "Paw," if you want your Rott to put his paw in your hand. Command her to "sit" as shown previously. Gently lift your dog's foot with your own hand as you say the word. Repeat this a number of times until you feel like she gets. Say, "Paw," again while showing her your open palm to see if she places her foot on your hand. Once she does, remember to generously reward her. This is not only a fun trick for your dog to know, it will also make clipping her nails faster and easier.

Discourage with a Firm "No"

This is perhaps one of the most important words that you can teach your Rottweiler. As mentioned in the earlier chapters, physical punishment and yelling are not good methods when it comes to training your dog. The best thing to do when attempting to discourage a dog from doing a bad behavior is to firmly say, "No." When teaching this word, use a lower tone of voice so they can learn to distinguish it from praise. You can also use the words, "Bad!" and "Stop!" to let your Rottweiler know that you don't approve of his behavior and that he should discontinue doing it. You can also try giving your dog a "time out" if he does something bad by keeping him on short leash or small enclosed space for a brief period of time. This also works to calm down aggressive behavior. If your dog fails to obey your command, just take him away from the situation and if he obeys, just continue your activities as usual.

"Down" Boy!

Rottweilers love to jump up and down, and they may even stand and lean on you! As they will inevitably get too big to do this, and this behavior will become especially undesirable with small children, you will need to teach your dog the word, "Down." Demonstrate the downward motion with your hands when you say the command. A note to dog owners: Your dog may confuse this command with sit, so it is better to teach this command later, after he has learned to sit.

"Stay"

This command is important if you wish your dog to stay in one place. He can either sit or lie down. "Stay" is different with "sit" and "down" because when you make this command it means that you want your dog to remain in one location and keep the same position for a longer period of time. It can also mean that you need him to remain in that same position and location until you finally give another command for him to "come." You can teach them to stay by getting them in the "sit" or "down" position, telling them to "stay", and then moving away from them with a treat in your hand. If they follow you, tell them "sit" or "down" again. Keep repeating this over longer and longer distances. Once they have satisfactorily performed the command "stay", walk towards them to give them the treat. "Stay" takes a longer time to learn and obviously, it is for more advanced Rotties that have already learned how to sit and lie down.

"Come"

After teaching your Rottweiler to "stay" you'll have fun calling out to her to "come." This command means she must go to you or follow you. While teaching this command you can use hand gestures to beckon your dog to approach you. You can also use whistling, clapping your hands together, or making sounds with your mouth. It is good to alternate practicing "stay" and "come" commands to make sure they associate the right action with the appropriate word and gesture.

Teaching your dog to follow your commands is crucial to their development. Rottweilers are working dogs by nature, so they are used to following commands in order to help their masters. These are obedient dogs, and while the process of teaching them can be tiresome and oftentimes frustrating, you will immediately feel rewarded when you witness your dog follow your command for the first time. It will no doubt encourage you to try another command. Just remember not to expect too much of your dog all at once. Make training as fun as possible for you and your dog, take your time, and never forget to reward your Rottie when she obeys your command.

Conclusion

You can always take the easy way out and hire a professional dog trainer to train your Rottweiler. However, this may result in your dog being more loyal to the person that trained them than they are to you. If it's possible, train your own dog and get the chance to create a special bond between you and your pet. Moreover, the services of professional dog trainers can be costly, so if you don't have the money to spare, then you should definitely train your own Rottie.

Rottweiler training is a long process that starts from the time your dog is a puppy and continues until he becomes a full-grown dog. Training does not stop at any point because you constantly need to teach your dog, reinforce his good behavior, and discourage him from bad behavior. Owning a Rottie is hard work and deciding to train him by yourself takes dedication, determination, and a whole lot of patience, so be sure that you are ready to take on the job. Sadly, many Rottweiler owners give up on training their dogs and a large number of Rotts are neglected, abandoned, or left in shelters.

Rottweilers are a loyal breed of gentle giants, and they need a lot of patience from their owners. If you want a tiny, low-maintenance dog, then get a Pomeranian or a Shitzu. Rottweilers are large dogs that need constant loving and attention. They are very devoted and protective of their owners. Training your Rottweiler takes a life-time of dedication, so you need to really love your Rottie for you to be able to train it well. A well-trained Rottweiler is a happy dog and a happy dog makes for a happy dog owner.

Finally, I'd like to thank you for purchasing this book! If you enjoyed it or found it helpful, I'd greatly appreciate it if you'd take a moment to leave a review on Amazon. Thank you!